Yes I Can

Overcoming self-imposed
limitations to live
your best life

MATT BIRD

Contents

Introduction

When you are asked, "What would your dream job or vocation be?" some people can become hyper-animated, energised and excited as they describe it. Then following on to ask, "So what is stopping you from pursuing what you would love to do?" The response is rarely money or know-how it is something within themselves.

I've had thousands of conversations about people holding back from a change of career, starting a business, committing to a relationship and beginning a community project. They hold back because on an inner obstacle.

I decided to write this book because I talk with many people about writing their book.

I coach more than 100 people a year to write, publish and launch their books to a global audience. Everyone of those people overcame one or more self-limiting beliefs in order to undertake a book adventure that transformed their lives.

There are many others however who simply can't seem to overcome their inner obstacles. I wrote this book to help more people overcome their self-limitations and write the book they have within them or start the business they have always dreamed of.

Whether you believe "Yes I Can" or "No I Can't" you are probably right! The game of whether we achieve or not is almost entirely won in our minds .

I left school believing I was stupid. I worked believing I was only suited for non-profit work. I lived believing I had to tone myself down. I have worked extremely hard to overcome each of these self-limitations in order to live my best life.

Day by day I am being transformed by the renewing of my mind and beliefs because lasting change takes place inside out not outside in—to the disappointment of the advertisers.

'Yes, I Can' explores ten self-limiting beliefs and how they hold us back. Most importantly it recommends practical strategies and personal affirmations to enable you to overcome negative beliefs. There is no silver bullet solution but rather an invitation to work every day to turn the dial on what we believe we can achieve and therefore we actually achieve.

'Yes I Can' will help you identify and understand your self-limitations. Enabling you to challenge incorrect convictions and develop new beliefs and thinking. Ultimately developing new behaviours, practices and habits.

The ten self-limiting beliefs are not mutually exclusive and neither are the practical strategies and personal affirmations. You can mix them up in whatever way works for you. Reading through the book beginning to end or choosing to read chapters that are of particular interest to you.

Here's to living more of the life you've dreamt of!

Chapter 1:

"I'm not ready"

Overcoming procrastination

How many times have you heard the words "I'm not ready"? It might be about starting a business, enrolling for a course or taking decisive action in another area of your life. I understand I've been there too.

I sometimes pause at the point of launching a new venture. I wonder, "Is this venture being driven solely by my personal passion or is there a genuine need for what I am creating?" It's a moment of stopping at the precipice beyond which there is no return and then jumping!

Procrastination... the act of delaying or postponing a task or action, often to the point of creating discomfort and negative consequences such as losing moments of opportunity.

"The future depends on what you do today, not tomorrow."
Mahatma Gandhi

A few years ago, my mum gave me a box. I opened it to discover that inside were my first pair of shoes. Even though I'm not known for sentimentality, it was an emotional moment. The shoes were made of blue leather with metal buckles on top, they are very cute.

When I looked at the shoes more closely I was disappointed because one of the shoes had a hole in the toe. Then the story behind the hole dawned on me: they were the pair of shoes I learnt to walk in. I had scuffed the toe so much it had worn through. They now sit in my studio as a reminder that each step is important no matter how faltering it may be and that ultimate success is the sum of many incremental steps.

One of the keys to overcoming procrastination is goal setting. Decide what your idea, desire or goal is and then take steps towards it every day. Stumbling and set backs are inevitable, it's a matter of getting up, standing on your feet and trying again and again and again until you achieve success.

You may find it helpful to follow my **goal builder model** by grabbing yourself a notebook and noting down your answers to these questions:

- What are the things that I really want to be, do or have? Write them down.

- Which are the most important to you? Write numbers beside each goal to indicate their priority in your life.

- When do you want to achieve your goals? Write a time deadline by each goal.

- Start with your most important goal and ask yourself, what are the sequence of steps that will enable me to achieve this goal? Write them down.

- You can repeat this for as many goals as you wish.

- Each day take at least one step towards each of your goals. Committing every day to taking at least one step toward each of your targets.

There is one thing you can do to put your goal setting and achievement on steroids... create accountability. Depending on the context of your goals, ask your partner, neighbour, boss, colleague, friend, mentor or coach for help. Explain the goal, timeline and steps which you have set and ask them to check in with you on an agreed frequency so that your can report progress made. This kind of accountability will dramatically increase the likelihood of you achieving your goal.

Action: If you suffer from a little procrastination, set goals and take steps towards them every day. Make yourself accountable to someone by agreeing to report your progress on a regular basis.

Yes I Can Affirmation...

"I'm going to do it now!"

Chapter 2:
"I can't do it"
Overcoming self-doubt

One of the most common self-sabotaging voices in your head can say, "I can't do it. I can't do it. I can't do it!"

The voice of doubt may only be a whisper but in a moment, that small voice has the ability to become completely immobilising. You no longer step forward, step out or step up; you are paralysed by self-doubt. As is described in an ancient book of wisdom the tongue can be likened to the rudder of a ship that whilst it is small it has the ability to change the direction of the ship.

Self-doubt... a type of negative self-talk or inner dialogue characterised by a lack of confidence in oneself. Excessive self-doubt can be debilitating and can prevent us from taking risks, pursuing our goals, or experiencing new opportunities.

"It is not the mountain we conquer but ourselves."
Sir Edmund Hillary

As a boy, I was part of a youth club and each week the first part of the evening would be time to hang out and the second part of the evening would be to take part in a game or activity. I remember like it was yesterday getting extremely frustrated with one of the activities and declaring, "I can't do it".

One of the youth leaders, a lovely lady called Jan, was within earshot and she immediately said, "There's no such thing as can't!" Those words have stuck with me to this day. Whenever I tell myself I can't do something, I hear Jan speaking back at me: there is no such thing as can't! Now a few decades on, I have learnt to believe it is true...there is no such thing as can't!

One of the keys to overcoming self-doubt is to practice manifesting which is the process of using positive thinking, visualisation techniques and affirmations to bring about your desired outcome. The idea behind manifesting is that by focusing thoughts and intentions on what you want to achieve, you can attract positive energy and opportunities that will help you make it a reality.

You might like to try a **manifesting methodology** this is one that I use personally and professionally:

- Close your eyes (after reading these steps!).

- Imagine your desired goal or dream future imaging all the details. Go through each of your senses asking: what will I see, what will I hear, what will I touch, what will I smell and what will I taste?

- Capture that state of being by taking a multi sensory photograph in your mind. Live out you dream using every sense.

- Create a physical vision board using a montage of photographs and images to illustrate your desired goal or dream future.

- Follow the goal-builder steps in the previous chapter to create a plan to work towards your desired goal or dream future.

- Look at your vision board daily or as often as you need to. Get into the right state of being.

Remember, manifestation only works if you do! You need to show up and put in the work.

Action: If you are filled with self-doubt about your ability to do something, remember there is no such thing as can't. Choose to manifest the reality of your desired goal or dream future.

Yes I Can Affirmation...

"There is no such thing as can't!"

Chapter 3:
"I'm going to fail"
Overcoming fear of failure

There are so many great sports to enjoy and there are probably seasons of life that go with them. I've had seasons of enjoying a variety of competitive sports including canoeing, squash, golf, cycling, badminton, clay pigeon shooting and spinning.

One of the fundamental things you learn if you play any sport, at anything more than a goofing around level, is the "inner game". The inner game is the understanding that any competitive game is won in your mind before it is won in the arena. This is known as sports psychology—whether you believe you are going to win, or lose the game, you are probably right.

Atychiphobia... or the fear of failure, is a phobia characterised by the belief you are going to fail. In extreme cases of this phobia, it interferes with your ability to to function and achieve your goals. People with atychiphobia may avoid taking risks or trying new things, and experience feelings of anxiety, self-doubt and inadequacy.

*"Failure is not the opposite of success;
it's a stepping stone to success."*
Arianna Huffington

The key is maintaining a winning mindset even when you've lost a point or are trailing behind. I know from painful experience that the minute you believe you are going to lose you begin to lose more quickly.

I often meet people who are deferring the pursuit of their dreams, whether it is to leave their job and start the business they have always dreamed of, or take the plunge to write the book that has always been a desire of their heart. Likewise, they may fear committing to a relationship, scared that it will go wrong. The primary reason they are deferring the pursuit of their dream is to avoid the possibility of failure and disappointment. If they don't expect or work to achieve their dreams then you cannot be disappointed by them.

This logic is actually self-defeating because avoiding the possibility of failure by avoiding the pursuit of your dreams results in even greater disappointment—the disappointment of never having tried to do what you dreamt of!

One of the keys to overcoming the fear of failure is reframing how you look at things. Reframing is a cognitive technique that involves looking at a situation or problem from a different perspective in order to change the way it is perceived or experienced.

One of the very simple **reframing techniques** that I use, which you may find helpful too, is to ask four questions:

- In this situation what is the worst that could happen?

- What is the best possible outcome?

- What is the high likelihood of the best outcome?

- Is likelihood of the best possible outcome worth the low risk of the worst outcome?

It involves shifting the focus away from negative or unhelpful thoughts and finding new, positive meanings that can lead to more effective outcomes.

For example, you can decide you will not fail again. If you accept that you will make mistakes (its inevitable) and view those mistakes as stepping stones to success, you will never fail again.

You may find it helpful to ask yourself, "What do I perceive success to look like?" Frame the picture in your mind using all your senses as you would do in your visualisation exercise. You may want to draw the picture in your mind or write it down. Then ask, "How can I use any deviation from this picture for my benefit?" Imagine a deviation, such as an apparent set back or failure, and reframe your picture to bring the distortion back into focus.

Action: If you struggle with fear of failure be mindful of what you allow yourself to think about. Reframe thoughts of the fear of failure into success.

Yes I Can Affirmation...

*"I am a winner and
I am winning."*

Chapter 4:
"I'm not worth it"
Overcoming low self-esteem

Ever look in the mirror in the morning, or any other time of day for that matter, and not like what you see? Having a low opinion of yourself—whether the way you look, the way you think or the things you do—is something all but the most erudite people in life wrestle with.

You may have an explainable or unexplainable reason for your low self-esteem. For example people with dyslexic often have low self-esteem. They may have been slow to read and write, or struggled with pronouncing and spelling words. These experiences can lead people with dyslexia to feel like they don't fit in and have low self-worth. And if those around them make them feel stupid it can be very damaging.

Low self-esteem... refers to a negative perception of yourself, characterised by feelings of inadequacy, inferiority, and self-doubt. People with low self-esteem often have a distorted view of themselves, seeing themselves as less capable, less likeable, or less worthy than others.

"You are stronger than you think, braver than you believe, and smarter than you know."
A.A. Milne

To say I struggled at school is a British understatement. I was placed in remedial Maths and English classes. I was told I couldn't do computer studies because my grasp of the English language wasn't strong enough. Consequently I left school believing I was stupid because that's what most of my teachers told me.

It took me years to overcome the belief that I was stupid. Whenever I couldn't do something, was turned down for an opportunity or rejected by someone, I told myself it was because I was stupid. It was a spiritual experience that most helped me to like and then love myself and caused my self-esteem to grow, thrive and flourish.

One of the keys to overcoming low self-esteem is self-love; the practice of accepting and caring for yourself unconditionally, without judgment or criticism. It involves developing a positive and compassionate attitude towards yourself, recognising and valuing your strengths, and treating oneself with kindness, respect, and forgiveness. Self-love is not about being selfish or arrogant, but rather about cultivating a healthy sense of self-esteem, self-worth and self-care. It involves taking care of your physical, emotional and spiritual needs, creating space for yourself and making choices that honour one's values and priorities.

One of the tools I use is to **self-date** as an expression of self-love... yes a date! Whether you're married or single you can self-date. If you like to plan you can work it out in advance or if you are spontaneous you can set aside the time and see what you feel like doing in the moment. It might mean going to a day spa, taking a train journey somewhere interesting, treating yourself to a restaurant meal or filling the bath, lighting candles, playing some music and popping open a bottle of bubbly. Have fun being creative about how you value, appreciate and look after yourself.

Action: If you feel like you are not good enough, take a moment to pause and remind yourself about your worth. Plan that date to show yourself some love!

Yes I Can Affirmation...

"I am absolutely fabulous!"

"I am unspeakably indebted."

Chapter 5:
"It's not good enough"
Overcoming perfectionism

"It's not good enough!" You may find yourself saying about an essay or assignment. Or a pitch, plan or project. Or an application for a business loan or charity grant. Or it could be that moment before you send the manuscript to your publisher for the book you have been writing for the last 100-days.

Perfectionism is extremely dangerous. As a human being you are imperfect - so how can someone who is imperfect make something that is perfect - it is impossible. Perfectionism is simply not achievable so think again.

Perfectionism.. a personality trait characterised by a high concern for perfection and a strong desire to achieve flawless performance. Perfectionists often set unrealistically high standards for themselves and others. They are often overly critical of mistakes or perceived shortcomings of themselves and others.

"Perfectionism is a twenty-ton shield that we lug around thinking it will protect us when, in fact, it's the thing that's really preventing us from taking flight."
Brene Brown

If you suffer with perfectionism then what I am about to say may give you heart palpitations. One of my life affirmations is that eighty per cent is good enough! You can get eighty per cent of the way to achieving what you want to in a relatively short amount of time. What would be required to get you to one hundred per cent of what you might like, will take you an incredible amount of time, energy and resources. In the vast majority of cases eighty per cent is enough!

Most of the time it isn't necessary or desirable to achieve one-hundred per cent, eighty per cent is good enough! So why bother killing yourself when enough is enough? Launch and learn rather than plan and perfect because progress is always better than perfectionism. Besides that, by the time you have planned and perfected, the moment you were planning and perfecting for may well have passed.

You may find it helpful to do a **cost-benefit analysis**, which is a decision making tool to decide whether to go ahead with a project. It is simply a list of pros and cons to help you decide the best thing to do.

List the costs and benefits of being eighty per cent right and then do the same for being one-hundred per cent right and compare the results. In particular think about the costs in terms of time, energy and money.

	80% Costs	**80% Benefits**
• Time		
• Energy		
• Money		

	100% Costs	**100% Benefits**
• Time		
• Energy		
• Money		

Are the additional costs and benefits of being one-hundred per cent perfect really worth it?

If your answer is yes, then do it! If not, then use your time, energy and resources differently.

One of the keys to overcoming perfectionism is to make a commitment to excellence instead of perfectionism. Excellence involves setting high expectations, standards and always pursuing learning and improvement. In addition, it also recognises that mistakes and imperfections are a natural part of being human and life.

People who pursue excellence are focused on growth and development, rather than solely on achieving perfect outcomes. They are resilient in the face of setbacks, and use mistakes as opportunities for learning and improvement. They are self-compassionate and do not judge themselves harshly for not meeting their own high expectations. They focus on the process of learning and growing, rather than solely on the end result.

Action: If you wrestle with perfectionism embrace the pursuit of excellence and accept that 80 per cent there is good enough.

Yes I Can Affirmation...

"Eighty per cent is good enough!"

Chapter 6:
"I can do it alone"
Overcoming excessive individualism

Come on we have all been there: we have all thought, "It's quicker to do it myself." Before we know it, that is exactly what we are doing—we are doing it all ourselves. We find ourselves living the lie that we are self-sufficient and believing that no one can do things as well as I can.

Recruiting, onboarding, developing, managing and leading a team takes time, energy and resources. And to build a high performing team even more is required of you. As people we are complicated creatures, each one unique and needs to be motivated and managed in different ways. Is it any wonder why some people decide to go it alone.

Excessive individualism... emphasises individual autonomy, independence and reliance, to the point of neglecting the needs and interests of team, organisation, community and society as a whole. This can manifest in a variety of ways, such as prioritising personal success over the common good, valuing individual achievement over collective progress, or failing to acknowledge the impact of your actions on others.

"Excessive individualism isolates us from the richness and diversity of human experience, narrowing our perspectives and limiting our growth."
Margaret J. Wheatley

One of the keys to overcoming excessive individualism is to understand the significance of relationships and our interdependence.

One of my chosen subjects of study is the art and science of relationships or what I call 'Relationology'. All the research evidences that the quality of our relationships determines our quality of life. Our well-being, whether our happiness, health or longevity of life, is impacted more than any other factor by the quality of our relationships. Our life opportunities, whether jobs, contracts or community activities, are determined by the depth and breadth of our interpersonal relationships. Our professional performance shows that relationships are the true currency and are the fastest, simplest and easiest way to get anything done.

Relationships are simply too important to leave to chance - so what is your relationship strategy? If you don't have one why not adopt the **Relationology strategy** which will help you be more intentional and deliberate about building relationships.

- **Collect Relationships:** How do you meet new people and add them into your relational ecosystem?

- **Keep Relationships:** How do you keep in contact with everyone you know? Recognising that you can't have the same relationship with everyone you know.

- **Grow Relationships:** How do you invest in deepening and strengthening your relationships?

If you would like to supercharge overcoming excessive individualism then discuss the matter with your coach or mentor. If you haven't got one, get one. Ask them to be your guide from the side line for joining, rather than initiating some collaborative projects.

Action: If you struggle with excessive individualism, take deliberate actions to become more collaborative. Get the accountability and help of someone alongside you.

Yes I Can Affirmation...

"The quality of my relationships determines my quality of life"

"The gravity of any relationship determines the gravity of loss"

Chapter 7:
"I'm not qualified"
Overcoming self-disqualification

You may talk yourself out of an opportunity by thinking you are unqualified, under qualified, over qualified or disqualified! You may decide that you are lacking education, training, experience, capabilities, license or authority.

The belief that you are not qualified is completely de-habilitating and can stop your advancement, progress and promotion dead in your tracks.

Self-disqualification... voluntarily Withdrawing from your application, candidacy or eligibility, or indeed to resign from your current responsibility or job.

*"Never let others disqualify your dreams.
Your belief in yourself is
what truly matters."*
Roy T. Bennett

I have often struggled to believe I am qualified for what I do, due to my upbringing, schooling and lack of a traditional 'career'. In my twenties, I studied for a Bachelors Degree, a masters degree and then a Masters in Business Administration. As I made enquiries about undertaking a doctorate I paused to check my motivation. Whilst I could have achieved a doctorate, I stopped because I realised there was no end to trying to qualify myself and I was in danger of that being my primary driver.

The key to overcoming self-disqualification is to understand that true qualification is not derived through external validation. No number of certificates, degrees or postgraduate qualifications from the most prestigious institutions would convince us we are qualified. True qualification only comes from within, a strong and deep conviction that we are suitable, fit and able.

Carrying a posture of life-long learning and never believing you have 'arrived' at your end point of learning is profoundly important. Life offers you formal and informal education experiences. Formal education through school, college, university and post graduate studies. Informal education through the 'university of life': the every day opportunities you have to grow and develop through people, places and the experiences around us.

You may find it helpful to use a **learning analysis approach** to see how qualified you are and also where there is scope to grow:

- **Formal Learning:** What are the top five things you have learnt through formal education?

- **Informal Education:** What are the top five things you have learnt through informal education?

- **Yet To Learn:** What are the top five things you would still like to learn?

It is important to remember that whilst learning is important, and in many professions critical, it is not these things that ultimately qualify us. Some people can have all the educational qualifications in work but still not believe, "Yes, I Can." A surprising number of entrepreneurs drop out of formal education because they struggle to fit in or because they just want to get going. They have an internal conviction about their ideas and enterprises that propels them forward, even when the going gets tough or they face what appears to be insurmountable obstacles. They believe they are qualified.

Action: If you want to overcome self-disqualification, recognise that its only you who can qualify or disqualify yourself from the game of life.

Yes I Can Affirmation...

"I am completely qualified"

Chapter 8:

"I don't have the resources"

Overcoming poverty mentality

Now I'm not going to kid you; I didn't grow up in poverty but things were very challenging. I remember hearing my parents talking and more often arguing about money. I didn't fully understand at the time, all I knew was that there was huge tension on this matter.

As a result of those strained financial times I grew up believing, "I can't afford that." Over the years, that belief became ingrained and was the knee-jerk reaction to opportunities for luxury expenditure, personal development or investment decisions.

Poverty mentality... a concern that there isn't enough to go around and even what you have now can be taken from you at any moment. Acquiring more is also beyond your reach.

"Poverty mentality is a self-imposed prison that limits our potential and keeps us from experiencing true abundance."
Robin Sharma

For a long time I have worked in the non-profit sector. In that world there was sometimes an odd expectation that you would learn to "walk with a limp". In other words, you had to give the impression that you were struggling to make ends meet. You should not present yourself as doing well otherwise it might be met with disapproval. It is a poverty mentality that creates this kind of worldview and behaviour.

One of the keys to overcoming a poverty mentality is to develop an abundance and generosity mentality. A mindset that emphasises the potential for growth, prosperity, and success. A mindset that gives generously to the people that you can help. People with an abundance mentality believe that there is plenty of opportunity and resources available.

You can genuinely create and attract more of what you want through positive thinking, hard work and collaboration.

Abundance focuses on solutions, possibilities, and opportunities, rather than on limitations, scarcity or lack. An abundance mentality leads to greater creativity, innovation, and resilience, and can help individuals to achieve their goals and live a more fulfilling life.

You may find it helpful to use my **abundance mentality framework** by intentionally thinking, speaking and operating on the left hand side rather than on the right hand side:

- Abundance vs Poverty Mentality
- Possibilities vs Limitations
- Opportunities vs Risk
- Offensiveness vs Defensiveness
- Growth vs Decline
- Solutions vs Problems
- Optimistic vs Pessimistic
- Plenty vs Scarcity
- Expansiveness vs Lack
- Create vs Maintain
- Collaborative vs Compete
- More vs Less

People who take a risk to create something out of nothing or make a lot with a little are entrepreneurs and nearly always have an abundance mentality. They believe anything is possible. Entrepreneurs know the only way to find out if an idea is going to work is to try it! I have always been hungry to stretch, grow and increase; so if the proverbial "door of opportunity" isn't knocking, then I make a door.

Action: If you would like to overcome a poverty mentality then embrace the abundance mentality strategy allowing your mind, words and actions to be transformed. You might even come up with an entrepreneurial idea and start taking steps to creating an abundance.

Yes I Can Affirmation...

"I am going to do it big"

Chapter 9:

"I'm too busy"

Overcoming busyness

If you are too busy to do what you want to do, it isn't your priority. Busyness is, without a doubt, one of the addictions of our time. It can consume us to the point of ineffectualness.

The demands on our time go on and on and on. Family, friends and colleagues. Home, work and social. Physical, mental and spiritual health. Earning, spending, saving, giving and investing money. The challenge is that the demands are most often legitimate so they can pull us to breaking point.

Busyness... the state of being fully occupied with tasks, activities and work. Being busy can be highly productive but it will more likely result in a lack of presence in the moment, induce stress and then burnout.

"

"Busy people often have the least time for the things that matter most."
Unknown.

Socially we are often asked, "Are you busy at the moment?". We are expected to say, "Yes!" The challenge is busyness is not a virtue, it is a vice. My answer to the question is, "I try to avoid being busy," and then laugh to soften the point. The person who asks knows exactly what I am saying. Busyness or lack of time is also used as a reason not to be able to do something new or different because there is a sense of being overwhelmed by what is already going on. This is a shame because it removes the possibility for something new, something fresh and something creative.

One of the keys to overcoming busyness or a sense of a lack of time is prioritisation. There is no such thing as a lack of time only a lack of priorities!

You may find it helpful to use my **time prioritisation tool** to enable you to work out the things that only you should be doing.

Start by writing down all the tasks that you feel you need to action and then run each task through the following set of questions and suggestions.

- **Eliminate:** Can I say "no" to this task?
- **Automate:** Can this task be automated?
- **Delegate:** Can I ask someone else to complete this task?
- **Schedule:** Can this task be scheduled for a convenient time?
- **Execute:** Action this task now!

In fact, every time a task demands that you action it, you can run it through these questions to ensure you maximise your personal effectiveness and productivity.

Once you have sorted out the tasks that you know you need to be doing, you can prioritise them into a list of 1-10.

As a result of becoming more focused and less busy, you will have more space and time in your life to think, reflect and rest. No matter how full life becomes, I try and take a working day every month to do nothing other than think and reflect. I'm amazed by the perspective on life, clarity of thought and the creativity of the ideas that these days stir within me.

Action: If you feel you are too busy, stop! Review all your goals, steps and tasks using the EADES model. Prioritise the stuff you really need to do. Now you have time and space to think, the most important of all the things we do.

Yes I Can Affirmation...

"There is no such thing as a lack of time only a lack of priorities"

Chapter 10:

"I'm going to get found out"

Overcoming imposter syndrome

The day your book is published, your first week in a new job or the moment you stand up to speak to an audience, shock waves can run through you.

We have all been there, a time when you find yourself doing something which you are seriously uncertain about whether you have the right to do. What if people find out?

Imposter syndrome... a psychological pattern in which you doubt your accomplishments. You live with a persistent concern of being exposed as a "fraud" despite evidence of your competence and success.

"The impostor syndrome doesn't go away, but you can learn to manage it by recognising when it's just noise in your head and pushing through it."
Michelle Obama

NAYBA, one of the ventures I started, helps churches better love their neighbourhoods. In virtually every way imaginable, I am not your usual community development candidate. Despite this, the foundation has grown to work in multiple countries across four continents. I have often wrestled with imposter syndrome because I think that any minute now, someone is going to blow the whistle on me and explain that I am a fraud. Yet, we have created with NAYBA really works for communities.

Recently, I caught up with a friend whose church I spoke at years ago. What he said surprised and delighted me. The speech I had given resulted in the church engaging with NAYBA had since started five projects helping people in the community who experienced vulnerability and isolation. Until that point, I had no idea of the impact, it helped me overcome my continued battle with imposter syndrome.

One of the keys to overcoming imposter syndrome is to both challenge and silence your negative self-talk and create and turn up the volume of your positive self-affirmations.

You may find it helpful to adopt **positive affirmation statements**...

- Take a piece of paper and write down your imposter syndrome beliefs.
- Take another piece of paper and write down positive affirmations that counter those beliefs.
- With great pleasure tear up and throw away your imposter syndrome beliefs.
- Declare these affirmations over yourself at the start of the day, if you struggle during the day declare them again.

For example this is what I have for each chapter of this book. I have taken a self-limitation and created an counter affirmation:

- I'm not ready - *Just do it!*
- I can't do it - *There is no such thing as can't.*
- I'm going to fail - *I am a winner and I am winning!*
- I'm not worth it - *I am absolutely fabulous!*
- It's not good enough - *Eighty per cent is good enough.*
- I can do it alone - *The quality of my relationships determines my quality of life*
- I'm not qualified - *I am completely qualified.*
- I am going to do it big
- I'm too busy - *There is no such thing as a lack of time.*
- I'm going to be found out - *I achieve because of my hard work and talents.*

Who you call yourself, how you describe yourselves and what you speak over yourself really does matter. You have worked and wrestled to be where you, doing what you are doing and you deserve it!

Action: If you want to overcome imposter syndrome talk to yourself differently. Prepare positive affirmations and think about and speak those things to yourself creating positive energy and vibes.

Yes I Can Affirmation...

"I achieve because of my hard work and talents"

Conclusion

I remember learning to swim. My dad had persuaded me to trust him and to splash around in the swimming pool with his support but without arms bands. All was going well until my sister jumped into what she thought was the shallow end. She couldn't swim a single stroke. Dad instinctively swam towards her but not before pushing me to the side of the pool. Unfortunately, I didn't quite make it to safety. In that moment, I discovered that if you want or need something bad enough, you'll find a way. In that moment I swam unaided for the first time.

Overcoming self-imposed limitations can sometimes happen in an instant because we simply have to. Other times it is like getting fit, you learn techniques, apply discipline and develop consistent habits in order to achieve long-term transformation.

Whether in an instant or through regular exercise the journey begins in your mind and extends to your body, words and actions so that everything within you says Yes I Can!

About Matt Bird

Matt Bird is a global speaker and entrepreneur.

He is CEO of Relationology providing relationship-centred business solutions to organisations wanting to grow by strengthening their relational capital.

Matt is also CEO of PublishU enabling over one-hundred people a year to write, publish and launch their books globally.

As part of his giving back Matt is Founder of NAYBA helping thousands of churches worldwide to better love their neighbours.

Matt has spoken in 50 countries to more than a million people, authored 20 books and writes for publications such as The Times newspaper.

He lives between Covent Garden in the heart of London's West End and Noto on the island of Sicily, Italy.

www.MattBirdGlobal.com

Printed in Great Britain
by Amazon

39669865R00069